A

Literature Unit

for

A

Christmas

Carol

by Charles Dickens

Written by Judith DeLeo Augustine

Illustrated by Keith Vasconcelles

Teacher Created Materials, Inc.
P.O. Box 1040
Huntington Beach, CA 92647
©*1993 Teacher Created Materials, Inc.*
Made in U.S.A.

ISBN-1-55734-434-5

Table of Contents

Introduction

The holiday season would not be complete without a visit from the three Christmas Spirits and the transformation of Scrooge. This unit for Charles Dickens' *A Christmas Carol* will allow students to experience Scrooge's story and examine their own ideas and beliefs about Christmas.

Since Dickens' vocabulary and sentence structure present a challenge to modern readers, the story has been introduced by dividing Section One into two parts, with separate Hands-On Projects, Cooperative Learning Activities, etc. It is strongly suggested that much of the reading be done orally with special attention to the rich, but probably unfamiliar, vocabulary. Teachers who use this unit will find the following features to supplement their own valuable ideas.

- Sample Lesson Plans

- Pre-reading Activities

- A Biographical Sketch and Picture of the Author

- A Book Summary

- Vocabulary Lists and Suggested Vocabulary Activities

- Chapters grouped for study, with each section including:

    - *quizzes*
    - *hands-on projects*
    - *cooperative learning activities*
    - *cross-curriculum connections*
    - *extensions into the reader's own life*

- Post-reading Activities

- Book Report Ideas

- Research Ideas

- A Culminating Activity

- Three Different Options for Unit Tests

- Bibliography

- Answer Key

We are confident that this unit will be a valuable addition to your planning, and we hope your students will gain a new understanding of Scrooge and Charles Dickens through these activities.

Sample Lesson Plan

Each lesson suggested below can take from one to several days to complete.

Lesson 1

- Complete pre-reading activities: discussion and worksheet. (page 5)
- Read "About the Author" with students. (page 6)
- Read the book summary with students. (page 7)
- Introduce vocabulary list for Section 1. Ask students to find definitions. Start vocabulary match game. (page 8)

Lesson 2: Section 1

- Read the beginning of Stave One; stop before Marley's visit. Place vocabulary words in context and discuss.
- Vocabulary Match Game. (page 9)
- Make Scrooge-style Christmas Cards. (page 11)
- Arrange study groups, complete the study group questions, and hold a class discussion. (page 12)
- Write Scrooge-style Christmas carols. Hold a sing-a-long. (page 13)
- Begin Reading Response Journals. (page 14)
- Administer Section 1 Quiz, Part 1. (page 10)

Lesson 3: Section 1

- Finish reading Stave One. Continue Vocabulary Match Game. (page 9)
- Plan a visit by an Unexpected Visitor. (page 11)
- Arrange study groups, complete study group questions, and hold class discussion. (page 12)
- Complete Community Research. Have students report findings to class. (page 13)
- Complete Reading Response Journals. Have students report findings about Personal Chains. (page 14)
- Administer Section 1 Quiz, Part 2. (page 10)
- Introduce vocabulary for Section 2. Ask students to find all possible definitions. (page 8)

Lesson 4: Section 2

- Read Stave Two. Discuss vocabulary in context.
- Continue Vocabulary Activities. (page 9)
- Discuss the flashback, setting changes, and visits.
- Complete the Journey Circle activity. Discuss.
- Have study groups complete questions and discuss.
- Explain how visualization can help one understand the story. Identify attributes of Spirit One. Have students draw illustrations. (page 18)
- Discuss differences between daily life in England in the 1800's and today. Complete research activity. Discuss similarities and differences. (page 19)
- Complete the Reading Response Journal. Have the students write about their past. (page 20)
- Administer Quiz for Section 2. (page 15)
- Introduce vocabulary for Section 3. Ask students to find all possible definitions. (page 8)

Lesson 5: Section 3

- Read Stave Three. Discuss vocabulary in context.
- Continue Vocabulary Activities. (page9)
- Make Plum Pudding. (page 22)
- Have study groups complete questions and discuss.
- Complete the visualization activity. Illustrate Spirit Two. (page 23)
- Complete Christmas Carol Code activity. (page 24)
- Complete Reading Response Journal. Have students write about their present lives. (page 25)
- Administer Section 3 Quiz. (page 21)
- Introduce vocabulary words for Section 4. Ask students to find all possible definitions. (page 8)

Lesson 6: Section 4

- Read Stave Four. Discuss vocabulary in context.
- Continue Vocabulary Activities. (page 9)
- Discuss Scrooge's glimpse into his future. Help students use imagination to see their futures. Complete the Crystal Ball activity. (page 27)
- Have study groups complete questions and discuss.
- Complete the visualization activity. Illustrate Spirit Three. (page 28)
- Organize public reading performance groups. Use "Lights! Camera! Action!" worksheet. Help students practice presentations. Arrange performance times.
- Complete Reading Response Journal. (page 30)
- Administer Section 4 Quiz. (page 26)
- Introduce vocabulary for Section 5. Ask students to find all possible definitions. (page 8)

Lesson 7: Section 5

- Read Stave Five. Discuss vocabulary in context.
- Continue Vocabulary Activities. (page 9)
- Plan a Christmas party. (page 32)
- Have study groups complete questions and discuss.
- Explain the math concept—tessellations. Have students design tessellated wrapping paper. (page 33)
- Complete Reading Response Journals. (page 35)
- Administer Section 5 Quiz. (page 31)

Lesson 8

- Discuss enjoyment and understanding of the book.
- Discuss the reading skill: cause and effect.
- Administer Unit Tests (option 1, 2, and/or 3). (pages 42-44)

Lesson 9

- Begin Culminating Activities in small groups or independently. Hold discussions and presentations if appropriate. (pages 39-41)

4

Before the Book

Activity One will help the teacher set the purpose for reading the book and relate author history to the novel. Activities Two and Three will allow the teacher to assess the students' background knowledge and also help identify any misconceptions about the story.

1. Brainstorm responses around the following questions:

   • What things—books, stories, celebrations, traditions—have lasted for a hundred years? (Answers may include the *U.S. Constitution, Declaration of Independence, Bible,* myths, schools, Halloween, etc.)

   • What things let you know the Christmas season has arrived? (Answers may include trees, ornaments, snow, bells, garlands, cards, etc.)

   • Why have such traditions and documents continued so long? (Suggest that they have wide appeal, giving people a sense of who they are and what they believe.)

2. Introduce the book, *A Christmas Carol.*

   • Ask the students if they are familiar with the story.

   • Ask if they know of the author or when the book was written.

   • Ask what causes a story to remain popular for over 100 years.

   • Explain the purpose behind the book—to persuade people to keep the Christmas spirit alive throughout the year by treating all with respect and kindness.

   • Explain that one benefit of literature is that the characters' situations help us to evaluate our own lives and question our own behaviors and ideas.

3. Have the students write down what they know about the book. After completion, share what is known. (You may wish to reproduce and enlarge the hat on page 9 for the students to write their responses on. Title it "What's Under Your Hat?")

   Following are some responses that might appear when students are asked to list what comes to mind upon hearing the title *A Christmas Carol.*

• Ghosts	• Horse-drawn carriages
• Large feasts, steaming food	• Lanterns
• Cold weather, snow	• Candles
• Gifts	• Old-fashioned houses
• Crippled children	• Formal clothes
• Christmas songs	• Poor people
• London	• Crabby old men

About the Author

Charles John Huffam Dickens was born on February 7, 1812, in Portsmouth, Hampshire in England. He was the second of seven children. A sickly child, he read books instead of playing with the other children. When Charles was ten years old, his father, John Dickens, moved the family to London. The family debts had become so great that their personal possessions were sold, and Charles was forced to leave school. In February, 1824, John Dickens was put in debtor's prison, and Charles, now twelve, began working at the Warren Blacking Factory gluing labels on bottles of shoe-blacking.

Dicken's writing career started at age fifteen. Through his own experience, he had developed a sincere concern for the poor and disadvantaged—especially children. Through his writing he helped his countrymen become aware of the effects of an industrialized society on all people. By February of 1836, his first collection of stories, *Sketches by Boz,* was published. With its publication, Dickens' career as a writer was confirmed.

A Christmas Carol was published in 1843. Dickens completed this book in a few weeks. Its simple message—keeping the Christmas spirit throughout the year—has made the story a timeless world classic. After the book's publication, the Christmas season changed dramatically in England. In 1843, the first Christmas cards were sold. Decorating trees and celebrating with family feasts became typical activities. Dickens' connection with Christmas was so great that when he died in 1870, people wondered if Christmas celebrations would also end.

Having always enjoyed acting and entertaining, Dickens began a series of public readings in 1858, always including *A Christmas Carol* in his performances. The readings were so popular that people paid $26.00 for a $2.00 ticket at his American debut. Unfortunately, these performances were also physically demanding. His final reading tour was abandoned when he collapsed in April, 1869. He died suddenly on June 9, 1870, and was buried in Westminster Abbey.

A Christmas Carol

by Charles Dickens

(Scholastic, 1987)
(Available in Canada, UK, and Australia through Scholastic)

A Christmas Carol is set in London, England in 1843; the time is Christmas Eve. We meet Ebenezer Scrooge, a miserly "man of business" without friends, unable to give or receive human kindness. Scrooge hates Christmas and all the sentiments of the season.

During the day, Scrooge is greeted by several Christmas well-wishers. His nephew Fred, his only relative, wishes Scrooge a Merry Christmas. Scrooge replies, "Bah. Humbug." He then dismisses two gentlemen collecting for the poor of the city. A small boy stops to brighten his day with a Christmas song. Angry, Scrooge picks up a ruler and chases the child away.

At the close of business, Cratchit, Scrooge's clerk, asks if he can have Christmas Day off. Scrooge reluctantly agrees, unhappy at paying a day's wages for no work in return. After eating Christmas Eve dinner alone, Scrooge is visited by the first of four supernatural spirits. His old business partner, Jacob Marley, returns from the grave to warn that Scrooge must change his earthly ways or suffer a terrible fate after death. Marley further explains that Scrooge will be visited by three spirits and urges him to pay attention to the message that each spirit brings.

The first spirit, the Ghost of Christmas Past, takes Scrooge on a journey into the past. He sees himself as a young boy, alone and friendless. He is reminded of his own apprenticeship. He sees his first love and regrets having left her behind to pursue his career. Feeling remorse for his actions, Scrooge begs the spirit to take him home.

His second visitor, the Ghost of Christmas Present, takes Scrooge through the city of London, showing him how the season's spirit has enriched the lives of all who accept it. The ghost takes Scrooge to Bob Cratchit's house where he sees Tiny Tim for the first time and learns of his illness.

The third and most frightening of all the ghosts is the Ghost of Christmas Yet to Come, confronting Scrooge with his own death and showing him there will be no one to mourn him or miss him when he is gone.

Waking on Christmas morning, Scrooge is a changed man. He vows to keep Christmas throughout the year and follow the lessons of the spirits. He becomes known as the man who could keep Christmas well.

Vocabulary Lists

On this page are vocabulary lists which correspond to each sectional grouping of *A Christmas Carol* as outlined in the table of contents. Ideas for activities using these words can be found on page 9.

Charles Dickens used a wide range of words in the English language, and studying his vocabulary broadens our own understanding and mastery of good literature.

Section One *(Marley's Ghost)*

unhallowed	executor	legatee	covetous	solitary
entreaty	trifle	implore	replenish	intimation
impropriety	resolute	lunatic	credentials	ominous
multitude	tremulous	rapture	congeal	caustic
		garret	misanthropic	

Section Two *(The First of the Three Spirits)*

opaque	recumbent	tunic	lustrous	conducive
reclamation	jocund	instantaneous	latent	laden
expend	transition	loath	condescension	decanter
tumult	capacious	deftly	corroborate	aspiration
		brigands	pillaged	

Section Three *(The Second of the Three Spirits)*

consolation	seething	demeanor	compulsion	intricate
glee	demurely	conspicuous	swarthy	bilious
subsequently	prematurely	shabby	ubiquitous	ensued
withered	goblets	exulted	blithe	dismal
		grog	abyss	

Section Four *(The Last of the Spirits)*

repute	disgorge	reek	slipshod	beetling
flaunting	repent	scanty	revered	avarice
beseech	relents	faltered	essence	tarry
inexorable	replete	foreshadow	intercede	strive
		repulse	dwindle	

Section Five *(The End of It)*

gruel	peals	jovial	loitered	poulterer
recompense	portly	pang	sidled	array
jiffy	feign	waistcoat	endeavor	borough
hearty	sealing wax	illustrious	amends	dispelled
		extravagance	giddy	

8

Vocabulary Activity Ideas

You can help your students master and retain the rich vocabulary used in *A Christmas Carol* by providing them with a variety of activities. Here are a few to try.

• Play Matching Hats. Each student makes two sets of hats. On one hat the student writes the word and on the other the definition. The number of hats the student needs will depend on the teacher. Each student may be responsible for a certain number of vocabulary words from the list or for the entire list. Hats may be made after each section so the students will have a complete set by the end of the novel. To play, all word hats are placed face up in a stack on the table. All the definition hats are spread out face up on the table. (The students will see one word card and all the definition cards.) The students working in pairs or small groups take turns matching words and definitions. If no one can match the given word with the definition, the word is placed at the bottom of the word pile. The one with the most matches at the end of the game is the winner. To increase the difficulty of the game, a time limit may be used.

• Compile a "Dickens Dictionary." To build your students' alphabetizing skill as well as learning new words, compile a class dictionary on chart paper or in composition books. As words are added, record and discuss alternative meanings and usage. Students will appreciate Dickens' mastery of our complex and flexible language.

• Compile a deck of synonym cards, using correct sentences that contain italicized words from the vocabulary lists—for example, "The gentlemen *implored* Scrooge to donate money to the poor." On the back, write three possible choices for a synonym—for example, *asked, ordered, begged.* Hold small team or individual challenges to identify the closest meanings.

• Practice correct word form. Provide sentences with blanks needing the correct form of a root word that appears at the end of the sentence—for example, "The gentlemen kept _____Scrooge to contribute money to help the poor of the city (implore)." Encourage students to use their dictionaries for help.

Quiz Time!

Part One: Before Marley's Visit

1. On the back of this paper, write a sentence or two describing Ebenezer Scrooge. Be sure you can support your ideas with events from the story.

2. List three things in Part One that prove the setting is England, 1843.

   _____

   _____

3. List the other characters in Part One. Explain each character's relationship to Scrooge.

   _____

   _____

4. Explain how Scrooge's lifestyle is inconsistent with his wealth.

   _____

   _____

5. Does Scrooge enjoy life? Use examples from the story to explain your answer.

   _____

   _____

6. Would you have wanted Scrooge to be your friend? Explain.

   _____

   _____

Part Two: Marley's Visit

1. Who is Marley? What is Marley's relation to Scrooge?

   _____

2. What is Marley's purpose in the story?

   _____

3. List several ways Marley and Scrooge are alike.

   _____

   _____

4. List several differences between Marley and Scrooge.

   _____

   _____

5. What signals does Dickens use to let the reader know that Scrooge will have an unusual evening?

   _____

Christmas Cards

Part One: Before Marley's Visit

In 1843, John Calcott Horsley created the first Christmas cards. The students will design Christmas cards they believe Scrooge would send to well-wishers.

Materials needed:

Construction paper, markers, colored pencils, crayons, scissors, and any other materials the teacher and students feel are appropriate. Some computer printing programs can also be used to print cards.

Lesson:

1. Discuss Scrooge's character traits and his feelings about Christmas.

2. Discuss the tradition of Christmas cards and the reasons people send them.

3. Direct the students to design Christmas cards that Scrooge would find appropriate to send. (At the end of the unit the students could design new Christmas cards that the changed Scrooge would send.)

An Unexpected Visitor

Part Two: Marley's Visit

Imagine you are Ebenezer Scrooge. Late one evening, you are surprised by an unexpected visitor, but you have one advantage Ebenezer did not have—YOUR VISITOR CAN BE ANYONE YOU CHOOSE! Select anyone you would like in the world, from any field— music, arts, sports, family members, historic persons, politics, etc.

1. Who would your visitor be? Why?

   _____

   _____

2. What questions would you ask?

   _____

   _____

3. List the refreshments you would serve.

   _____

   _____

4. What activities would you plan?

   _____

   _____

5. How would you prove to others that this person had really visited you?

   _____

Study Group Questions

When studying a complex novel such as *A Christmas Carol*, the teacher may wish to organize small discussion groups. Questions and activities for such groups are provided in each section of the novel. (See also pages 18, 23, 28, and 33.) After the groups have completed their activities, a whole group sharing session may be held.

Section 1, Part One: Before Marley's Visit

1. List five character traits of Scrooge. Provide evidence from the story to support your ideas.

   _____

   _____

   _____

2. What is valuable to Scrooge? _____

3. How would you explain the importance of the Christmas season to Scrooge?

   _____

   _____

   _____

4. Prediction: How did Scrooge get his unusual attitude toward Christmas?

   _____

   _____

Section 1, Part Two: Marley's Visit

1. What was the purpose of the ringing bell? _____

   _____

2. Why did Marley visit Scrooge? What does this visit tell us about Marley?

   _____

   _____

   _____

3. What does Marley's chain represent? How is the chain made? _____

   _____

   _____

4. What frightens Scrooge the most in this section? _____

   _____

5. Explain Marley's fate. What does Marley explain to Scrooge about his never-ending journey?

   _____

   _____

6. What does Scrooge learn from Marley? _____

   _____

Christmas Carols, Scrooge-Style

Part One: Before Marley's Visit
Activity:

1. Discuss Scrooge's character traits and his feelings about Christmas.

2. Discuss the purpose of writing and singing Christmas carols. Play several commonly known carols to refresh the students' memories of the words and melodies.

3. Direct the students to rewrite a Christmas carol that would please Ebenezer Scrooge's taste in Christmas music. The students can use the same melodies and some of the word structures, but they will need to make several changes to reflect Scrooge's Christmas feelings. (These songs can be completed by individuals or small groups.)

4. The students should perform their songs for the rest of the class.

Community Research

Part Two: Marley's Visit

In the beginning of the book, Scrooge is visited by two gentlemen who are collecting for the poor. In this section, Marley explains to Scrooge that it is everyone's duty to help other people. By giving to others, we enrich our own lives.

1. What holiday activities are being done for the needy in your community?

2. Is there some way you could get involved with these efforts?

3. Places to contact: city hall, park district, churches, clubs, schools, businesses, etc.

4. Write a report about the activities in your community and what you can do to help the efforts to bring holiday happiness to others.

Reading Response Journal

One way to see that *A Christmas Carol* touches each student in a personal way is to include the use of Reading Response Journals. The purpose of the journal is to record thoughts, ideas, observations, and questions as we read. To stimulate writing, introduce the topics suggested for each section of the story, discuss, and ask the students to respond in their journals. Also, things newly learned, questions, and diary-type responses may be included.

Christmas Traditions *(Section 1, Part One: Before Marley's Visit)*
- Student Question: "Where do our Christmas traditions come from?"
- Review the story and discuss the topic.
- Develop a list of Christmas traditions in your school, community, and our country.
- Respond to the question.

    1. List three of your family's traditions.

        _____

        _____

        _____

    2. Explain the origin of each tradition.

        _____

        _____

        _____

Your Personal Chain *(Section 1, Part Two: Marley's Visit)*
- Student Question: "How long is your chain?"
- Review the story and discuss the topic.
- Respond to the question.

    1. List all the good deeds you were involved in during the week.

        _____

        _____

        _____

    2. Explain what you did, who benefited, and how you felt about your actions.

        _____

        _____

        _____

Extension: Prepare a paper chain individually or as a class. Write a good deed and the doer's name on each link.

Quiz Time!

1. Using complete sentences, carefully describe the appearance of the first Spirit.

   _____

   _____

   _____

2. The Spirit shows Scrooge his own past loneliness as a child whose only friends were characters in books. Scrooge feels a pang of sorrow and sheds a tear, for he connects the scene with something that had happened earlier that day. It causes him deep regret. Can you describe what had happened, why he is sorry, and what he wishes he had done?

   _____

   _____

   _____

3. The Spirit next shows Scrooge with his sister and says, "...she had a large heart." What does he say next that causes Scrooge to feel uneasy in his mind?

   _____

   _____

   _____

4. The Spirit next shows old Fezziwig holding a joyous Christmas party and dance. Scrooge was a young apprentice then and is delighted to remember his old employer's generous actions. The Spirit questions whether Fezziwig deserves praise, and Scrooge defends him, saying, "...the happiness he gives is quite as great as if it cost a fortune."

   His own words make Scrooge instantly remember and regret an action earlier in the day. What had happened, why is he sorry, and what do you think he wishes he had done?

   _____

   _____

   _____

5. The Spirit shows Scrooge a final scene from the past—Belle, the girl he had once loved but lost because of his greed. Using complete sentences and specific details, describe the events in Belle's home on Christmas Eve.

   _____

   _____

   _____

A Journey Circle

Where did Scrooge go? What did he see?

Activity:

1. Dickens writes this section of the book as a flashback. Explain flashback (as an author's tool) to the students and examine why it is important to the story for Scrooge to relive his past.

2. Review with the students the places Spirit One shows Scrooge—his boarding school, apprentice shop, the last meeting with his former girlfriend, and his former girlfriend's home.

3. Explain that each location has a significance to the Spirit's lesson and a profound effect on Scrooge.

4. Duplicate the Journey Circle worksheet on page 17 for students to use.

5. Students will complete the Journey Circle by writing and illustrating the places Scrooge and the Spirit visit and explaining the effect each place has on Scrooge. (Note to the teacher: This worksheet could be completed by individual students as a quiz or by small groups as a way to help one another clarify the author's message.) See sample below.

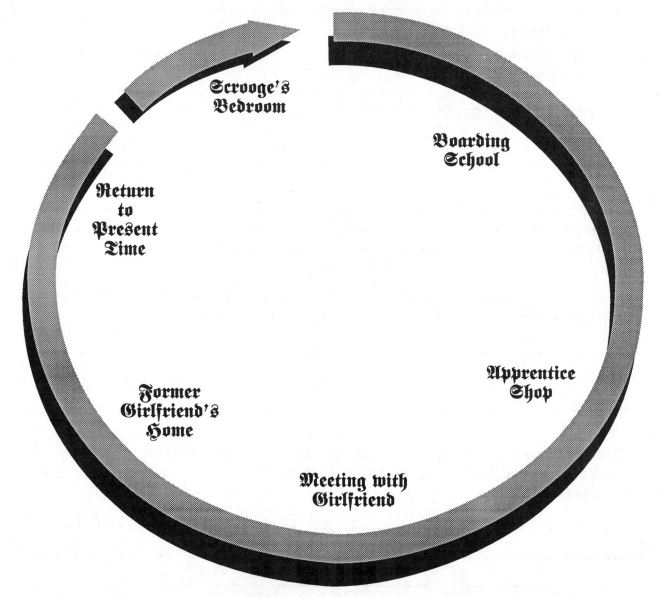

Journey Circle

Directions: Illustrate Stave Two of the novel by showing the places visited by Scrooge and the spirit (in sequence) on the circle. Write several sentences to explain the importance of each place to the Spirit's lesson.

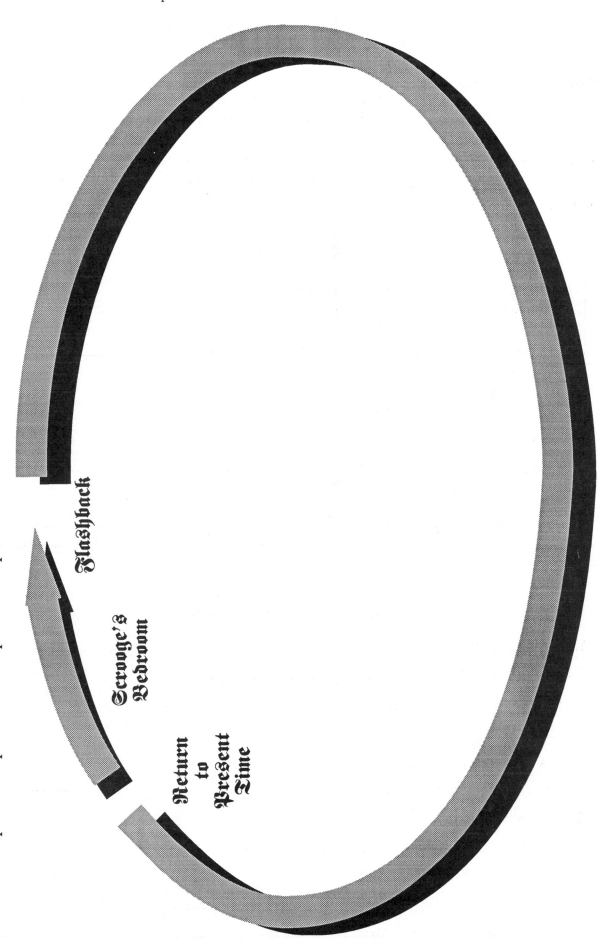

Flashback

Scrooge's Bedroom

Return to Present Time

Study Group Activities

See directions on page 12.

Section 2: The First of the Three Spirits

1. Explain what the Spirit's light represents. _____
   _____

2. What would cause the Spirit to hide its light under its cap? _____
   _____

3. Why did the Spirit visit Scrooge? What was Scrooge's initial reaction to the Spirit?
   _____
   _____

4. How did young Scrooge change throughout his life? _____
   _____

5. What may have caused Scrooge to turn his attitude toward gold and away from people? _____
   _____

6. List the things in his past that caused Scrooge's present attitude about Christmas.
   _____
   _____

Author Craft—Vivid Vocabulary

The following activity may be completed after each Spirit section is read. The purpose is to examine unusual vocabulary, analyze descriptive phrases, and evaluate the significant characteristics of each Spirit. For the first Spirit the teacher should guide and model the activity using the following steps.

- Discuss the importance of the author's use of vivid language.

- Read orally the description of Spirit One. Ask the class to visualize the Spirit as they listen.

- Identify any unknown words in the passage. Have students use dictionaries to define them.

- Identify and list the critical attributes of Spirit One.

- Working in groups, students should illustrate the Spirit. The illustrations must be based on the written description. Make the drawings large and colorful.

- Explain the links between the Spirit's characteristics and its message.

Comparing Past to Present

Dickens' book presents us with a picture of daily life as it was in England in the 1800's. Many of the activities are similar to our activities today. Using the novel as your reference source, write details to complete the following chart. (If necessary, dictionaries and encyclopedias may be used to check the meanings of unknown words.)

Category	Then	Now
Clothing		
Occupations		
Apprentices		
Education/Schools		
Transportation		
Stores/Shops		
Entertainment/ Celebrations		
Music		
Foods		

Reading Response Journal

Reading stimulates our thoughts, ideas, observations, and questions. When we record those reactions in a journal, we deepen our knowledge, clarify our thoughts, and preserve our love for the book. Here is one sample reading response topic from *A Christmas Carol*.

Your Past

- Student Question: "Which events of your past have affected your present?"

- Review the story and discuss the topic.

- Respond to the question.

    1. Think about past experiences, family activities, moves to new schools, vacations, personal accomplishments, etc.

    2. Have these events helped you develop interests, activities, or hobbies? Have any people helped you to understand yourself or to deal with friends and form relationships?

    3. List the events which have affected your present.

        _____

        _____

        _____

        _____

        _____

    4. Explain how the events have affected your life.

        _____

        _____

        _____

        _____

        _____

        _____

        _____

        _____

        _____

        _____

        _____

Quiz Time!

1. Using complete sentences and specific details, describe the Ghost of Christmas Present.

    _____

    _____

    _____

2. What physical change has taken place in the Ghost by the end of Stave Three?

    _____

    _____

3. The Ghost and Scrooge visit Bob Cratchit's home. Using complete sentences and specific details, describe the home, the children, and the dinner.

    _____

    _____

    _____

4. The Ghost next takes Scrooge to visit Fred, his nephew. Using complete sentences and details, describe the activities that take place there. _____

    _____

    _____

5. Scrooge sees that he is being discussed at both Cratchit's and Fred's homes.

    a. Explain carefully how Bob Cratchit refers to Scrooge. What does he say?

        _____

        _____

    b. What does Mrs. Cratchit say about Scrooge?

        _____

        _____

    c. Explain carefully how Fred refers to Scrooge. What does he say?

        _____

        _____

    d. What does Fred's wife say about Scrooge?

        _____

Plum Pudding

The Pride of the Christmas Dinner

In half a minute Mrs. Cratchit entered—flushed, but smiling proudly—with the pudding, like a speckled cannonball, so hard and firm, blazing in half-a-quartern of ignited brandy, and bedight with Christmas holly stuck into the top.

The highlight of the Christmas dinner and a source of pride to English cooks in the 1800's, plum puddings were dark, moist, and full of fruit. Surprisingly, they did not contain plums. They resembled fruitcakes. The family took turns stirring the mixture while making a wish with each turn. The pudding was steamed for several hours and stored for several weeks before it was served on Christmas. Due to the complexity of the original recipe, a modern microwave version is included here.

Cherry Pudding

Ingredients:

- 16 oz. (500mL) can pitted bing cherries, drained and cut into quarters
- ½ cup (120mL) water
- ¼ cup (60 mL) apple juice
- ½ teaspoon (2.5 mL) vanilla
- ¼ cup (60 mL) mild molasses
- 2 eggs
- 1 pkg. quick bread mix
- ½ teaspoon (2.5 mL) nutmeg
- ½ cup (120 mL) chopped nuts

Directions:

1. Grease microwave-safe bowl (4 cup—1 L), cover bottom with waxed paper and grease again.

2. In a mixing bowl, combine water, apple juice, vanilla, molasses, and egg.

3. Add bread mix, cherries, nutmeg, and nuts.

4. Stir until well mixed—50 to 75 strokes.

5. Pour 2 cups (500 mL) of the batter into the prepared bowl; tightly cover with plastic wrap.

6. Microwave on medium setting for 9 to 11 minutes; halfway through cooking, rotate pudding ¼ turn.*

7. Cooking is complete when center top springs back when lightly touched and pudding pulls away from sides of bowl.

8. Remove plastic wrap, and allow to stand for 5 minutes.

9. Before inverting onto serving dish, loosen pudding from sides of bowl.

10. Remove waxed paper.

11. Cook remaining batter.

* Cooking times may vary.

Study Group Activities

See directions on page 12.

Section 3: The Second of the Three Spirits

1. Why is the Ghost of Christmas Present a stranger to Scrooge? _____
   _____

2. Where does the Ghost of Chrismas Present take Scrooge? _____
   _____

3. Why did the Spirit not show Scrooge his own present Christmas? _____
   _____

4. Bob Cratchit offers a Christmas toast in Scrooge's honor. Mrs. Cratchit's feelings about Scrooge are different from her husband's. What would cause this difference in their feelings?
   _____
   _____
   _____

5. After visiting the celebrations at the Cratchit's house and at his nephew's house, how do Scrooge's attitude and feelings begin to change? _____
   _____

6. What is happening to the Spirit at the end of this section? What would cause this to happen?
   _____
   _____
   _____

Author Craft—Vivid Vocabulary

- Identify and list the critical attributes of Spirit Two.

- List any terms new to you. Use a dictionary to define them.

- As a group, illustrate the Spirit and explain all links between its attributes and the Spirit's message.

   _____
   _____
   _____
   _____
   _____

Christmas Carol Code

During his life Charles Dickens witnessed a number of scientific advances. The first electric motor, the first typesetting machine, the world's first railway, the revolver, the sewing machine—all these were developed in the years between 1812 and 1870. Perhaps most important of all was the invention of the telegraph. In 1844—a few short months following the publication of *A Christmas Carol*—Samuel B. Morse sent the first message over a line connecting Baltimore and Washington. By the end of the 1850's, most large cities of America and Europe were connected. Well before Dickens' death, messages were moving from England to America over transatlantic cable. For over a century now, Morse's ingenious system of dots and dashes has been used, first by telegraphers and then by radio operators to communicate all over the world. The following version is known as the International Morse Code. (The best known Morse message is ...---... Do you know what it stands for?)

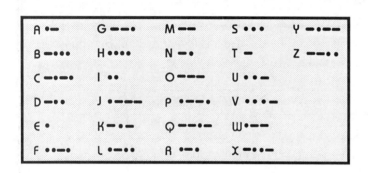

A •—	G ——•	M ——	S •••	Y —•——
B —•••	H ••••	N —•	T —	Z ——••
C —•—•	I ••	O ———	U ••—	
D —••	J •———	P •——•	V •••—	
E •	K —•—	Q ——•—	W •——	
F ••—•	L •—••	R •—•	X —••—	

Activity 1: Decode the following message from *A Christmas Carol*.

•— —• ••• / ••• ——— / •— ••• / — •• —• —•—• / — •• —— / ——— —••• ••• • •—• •••• — • —••/

——• • ——— —••/ —••• •—•• • ••• ••• / ••— ••• / • •••• — • •—• —•— / ——— —• •

Activity 2: Write in International Morse Code the following passage from *A Christmas Carol*.

'Bah!' said Scrooge. 'Humbug!'

_____

_____

Activity 3: The following words appear in "The First of the Three Spirits."

'A solitary child neglected by his friends is left there still.'

Answer the following questions in International Morse Code.

A. Who spoke these words? _____

B. Who was the character speaking to? _____

C. Who was the "solitary child"? _____

D. Print your name. _____

E. Now print your name in code. _____

Reading Response Journal

Reading stimulates our thoughts, ideas, observations, and questions. When we record those reactions in a journal, we deepen our knowledge, clarify our thoughts, and preserve our love of the book.

Topic: This is Your Life

- Student Question: "Through Spirit One, Scrooge is given an opportunity to relive his life. Through Spirit Two, Scrooge is able to witness his acquaintances as they talk about him. Would you like this opportunity? Explain."

- Review the story and discuss the topic.

- Respond to the question.

1. Would you like the same opportunity that was given Scrooge? _____

2. Explain your answer.

_____

_____

_____

_____

_____

_____

_____

_____

_____

_____

_____

_____

_____

_____

_____

_____

_____

Quiz Time!

1. Using complete sentences, explain the lesson that Scrooge learns from each Spirit.

   Spirit One:

   _____

   _____

   Spirit Two:

   _____

   _____

   Spirit Three:

   _____

   _____

2. What was Dicken's purpose in presenting the Spirits in time order (past, present, future)?

   _____

   _____

   _____

3. Which Spirit was the most frightening to Scrooge? Explain your choice.

   _____

   _____

   _____

4. Which Spirit had the greatest effect on Scrooge? Explain your choice.

   _____

   _____

   _____

5. Choose one of the Spirits. Describe it. Explain how its appearance relates to its lesson.

   _____

   _____

   _____

   _____

   _____

   _____

What Do You See in Your Future?

Spirit Three gives Scrooge a glimpse of his future. Using your mind's eye and your imagination, what do you see in your future?

Part One:

Organize your thoughts by completing the following worksheet.

1. Where do you live? Are you in a big city, the country, near the ocean or mountains? What country do you live in?

    _____

2. Are you living in a house or an apartment?

    _____

3. Who are your friends? Why did you choose them for your friends?

    _____

    _____

4. How do you make a living? What career did you choose? What made you decide to work in that field?

    _____

    _____

5. What is your family like? Are you married or single?

    _____

6. What transportation do you use each day? (car, plane, train, other)

    _____

7. Where did you go to school? Did you attend college? Have you received any awards?

    _____

    _____

8. What are your hobbies? How do you have fun?

    _____

    _____

Part Two:

On a separate sheet of paper, write a paragraph describing your future. In order to make your vision of the future clear, use complete sentences and include the details written above.

Study Group Activities

See directions on page 12.

Section 4: The Last of the Spirits

1. Scrooge says, "I am not the man I was." What does he mean? What causes the change? How do the Spirits cause the change in Scrooge? _____

    _____

    _____

2. What does this final experience teach Scrooge? _____

    _____

    _____

3. Why is Stave Four the most frightening for Scrooge? Why is the future more frightening than the present? _____

    _____

    _____

4. Explain why the visions of the future would convince Scrooge to alter his life.

    _____

    _____

5. At the end of this section, Scrooge promises to honor Christmas all year. How does Scrooge see this promise as a way to alter his present life? _____

    _____

    _____

6. Do you think Scrooge would have changed his life without the help of the Spirits? Explain your answer.

    _____

    _____

    _____

Author Craft--Vivid Vocabulary

- Identify and list the critical attributes of Spirit Three.

- List any terms new to you. Use a dictionary to define them.

- As a group, illustrate the Spirit and explain all links between its attributes and the Spirit's message.

    _____

    _____

    _____

Lights! Camera! Action!

Dickens enjoyed entertaining throughout his life. Between 1858-1870, his public readings were very popular. A passage from *A Christmas Carol* was always included in these performances. Students may also participate in public readings using a few simple props and the novel text as a script.

Cast:

Students should be placed in groups of three. One student will be the narrator, one student will be Scrooge, and one student will be Spirit One, Two, or Three.

Script:

The narrator will be responsible for a prologue to set the scene and an epilogue to finish the story for the audience. Each group will work together to decide what the narrator's script should include. The narrator should also read the descriptive details needed for the audience to visualize what the Spirit shows Scrooge. Scrooge and the Spirit should read the dialogue from the novel.

Costumes and Props:

Costumes should be very simple. (Public readings were not stage productions.) The narrator could dress much like Scrooge or Cratchit. However, Scrooge is in nightwear during meetings with the Spirits. The Spirit costume should follow the descriptions, using only the most important features.

Scenery:

Scenery was not used in public readings. The audience visualized the scenes, and the readers used their voices to convey the emotions. Simple stage movements may be used to help the audience understand the story.

Performances:

Performances could be given to other classes throughout the school. Each performance should be limited to one Spirit scene so the narrator's prologue and epilogue have meaning to the audience.

Reading Response Journal

Reading *A Christmas Carol* stimulates our thoughts, ideas, observations, and questions. When we record those reactions in a journal, we deepen our knowledge, clarify our thoughts, and preserve our love for the story.

Topic: Your Future

- Student Question: "Scrooge is frightened by the visions of his future. When you think about your future, how do you feel--nervous, excited, scared, confident, eager...? Explain your feelings."

- Review the story and discuss the topic.

- Respond to the question.

    1. How do you feel about your future?

    _____

    2. Explain your hopes, concerns, plans, feelings.

    _____

    _____

    _____

    _____

Topic: New Year's Resolutions

- Student Question: "Scrooge promises a new life in the future. People use New Year's Day as a time to examine their lives and decide on areas they would like to improve. Think about your own life. What New Year's Resolutions would you like to follow throughout the coming year?"

- Review the story and discuss the topic.

- Respond to the question.

    1. What New Year's Resolutions would you like to follow?

    _____

    _____

    2. How could you ensure that you would follow them?

    _____

    _____

Quiz Time!

1. List several changes in Scrooge.

   _____

   _____

   _____

2. Besides changes in Scrooge, what other changes does Dickens include in this section?

   _____

   _____

   _____

3. Why were the Spirits able to change Scrooge's attitude?

   _____

   _____

   _____

4. How does Scrooge show he is sincere about his promise to keep Christmas all year?

   _____

   _____

   _____

5. Predict what Scrooge's future life will be like.

   _____

   _____

   _____

   _____

6. Would you want the new Scrooge for a friend? Explain your answer.

   _____

   _____

   _____

Let's Party

Dickens loved Christmas time, and celebrations were often featured in his writing. By describing Fred's party in Stave Three, Dickens gives a complete look at entertaining in England in the 1800's. Review Stave Three of the novel and list all the details of Fred's party.

- Music: _____
- Games and activities: _____
- Foods: _____
- Other details: _____

Activity One: Plan your most extravagant dream party. (individual assignment)

- Where will it be held? _____
- Who will provide entertainment? _____
- How will the room be decorated? _____
- What refreshments will be served? _____
- What activities will be planned? _____
- Who will be on the guest list? _____
- Design a poster-sized invitation to be displayed in the classroom. It should be colorful and explain all details of the party.

Activity Two: Plan a realistic class celebration. (group assignment)

1. Select Committee Members

   - Entertainment: _____
   - Decoration: _____
   - Activities: _____
   - Refreshments: _____
   - Clean up: _____

2. Planning Guide

   - Where will it be held? _____
   - Who will provide entertainment? _____
   - How will the room be decorated? _____
   - What refreshments will be served? _____
   - What activities will be planned? _____
   - Who will be on the guest list? _____

Study Group Questions

See directions on page 12.

Section 5: The End of It

1. Specifically, what did Scrooge learn from each Spirit?

   Past: _____

   Present: _____

   Future: _____

2. At the beginning of Stave Five, Scrooge is happy that the "time" before him is his own. Why would time be so important to Scrooge?

   _____

   _____

3. How has Scrooge changed?

   _____

   _____

4. Explain the new feelings Scrooge has for the door knocker.

   _____

   _____

5. Define the word *blithe*. Write three synonyms for *blithe*.

   _____

   _____

6. Why was Scrooge so pleased with all the sights and sounds of Christmas?

   _____

   _____

7. Fred and Bob Cratchit have two different initial reactions to the new Scrooge. Explain why the men react differently.

   _____

   _____

   _____

Tessellation Holiday Style

The new Scrooge has embraced Christmas and all of its traditions. The practice of gift giving in England of the 1800's did not resemble today's tradition. Today the gift's wrapping is almost as important as the present itself. By using geometry and the idea of tessellation, the students will design colorful Christmas wrapping paper.

Materials needed:

scissors, colored pencils, rulers, white drawing paper, wallpaper or wrapping paper sample that shows a repeating pattern

1. Using paper samples, ask the students to identify what is repeated in the design on the paper. (color and shape)

2. Explain that a tessellation is a pattern that is made by the repetition of a shape that has been flipped or turned onto itself. The shapes can be altered and made to fit into one another like a puzzle. The shapes cannot overlap, and there should not be any spaces between the shapes. Exact tessellation patterns are complicated to make because the original pattern piece is cut and altered to make puzzle pieces that fit together in a precise way.

3. Examine the sample papers to identify the ways the designers repeated the patterns: stripes, blocks, upside down flip, sideways slide, etc.

4. Assign: Design your own Christmas wrapping paper. Be creative and original in your thinking. Choose a pattern and repeat it in some way so the paper will resemble a tessellation pattern. Make the paper suitable for a Christmas gift. Simple Christmas shapes can be provided for the students to help them in the planning of their own wrapping paper designs. Examples: bells, stars, trees, canes, etc.

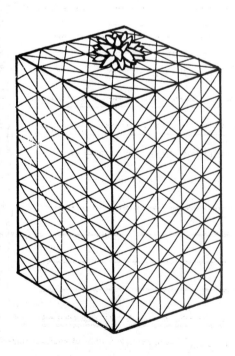
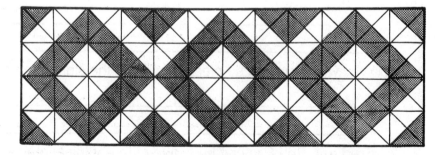

Reading Response Journal

Reading *A Christmas Carol* stimulates our thoughts, ideas, observations, and questions. When we record our reactions in a journal, we deepen our knowledge, clarify our thoughts, and preserve our love for the story.

Topic: Keeping Christmas All Year

- Student Question: "If we learn anything from Scrooge's experience with the Spirits, we now understand it is important to 'keep Christmas well' throughout the year. Explain how you will keep the Christmas spirit alive throughout the year."

- Review the story and discuss the topic.

- Respond to the question.

  1. How will you keep the Christmas spirit well throughout the year?

  _____

  _____

  _____

  _____

  _____

  _____

  _____

  _____

  _____

  2. Do you think this will be a difficult thing to do? Explain.

  _____

  _____

  _____

  _____

  _____

  _____

  _____

  _____

  _____

Any Questions?

When you finished reading *A Christmas Carol,* did you have some questions that were left unanswered? Write your questions here.

_____

_____

_____

Work alone or in groups to prepare possible answers for the questions you asked above and those written below. When you finish your predictions, share ideas with the class.

1. Did Tiny Tim ever grow up to be healthy? Did he always need a crutch? Did new medical discoveries help him? If so, how? What becomes of him?

2. Did Topper and the plump sister ever get married and have a family? What names would they give their children? What becomes of them? Does Scrooge become their friend?

3. When Scrooge retires, what becomes of his business? Where will he go when he retires? He has no family, so what will he do? What finally happens to him?

4. What happens if Scrooge ever returns to visit Belle's family? How does she react? What does her husband do and say? How do the children react to Scrooge? Does he bring gifts? Do they all react the same to the changed man?

5. What happens to Martha and Belinda? What kind of career does Peter make for himself? Is he successful?

6. Scrooge decides to change his interior decoration after Christmas. Describe how he will change the appearance of his rooms.

7. Dickens loved to give expressive names to his characters like Scrooge, Old Fezziwig, Tiny Tim, and Belle (which means beautiful). He does not say what Fred's last name is, however. Propose what you think might be several good last names for Fred, the nephew who loved to laugh and make people happy. Explain your choices.

8. Suppose Scrooge wants to express his thanks to Marley for making him a changed man. How will Scrooge try to do this? Will it be successful? If you were to write a story, what would you have Scrooge do?

9. Can "ghosts" from your past (memories, regrets, kindnesses, accidents) actually affect your present or future behavior? Explain.

10. How old does Scrooge live to be? Describe his funeral, the people who attend, and what they say.

Book Report Ideas

There are numerous ways to report on a book. After you have finished reading *A Christmas Carol*, choose one method of reporting that interests you. It may be a way that your teacher suggests, an idea of your own, or one of the ways below.

• See What I Read?

This report is a visual one. A model of a scene from the story can be created, or a likeness of one or more of the characters from the story can be drawn or sculpted.

• Time Capsule

This report provides people living in future time with the reasons *A Christmas Carol* is such an outstanding book and gives these "future" people reasons it should be read. Make a time capsule design and neatly print or write your reasons inside the capsule. You may wish to hide your capsule after you have shared it with your classmates. Perhaps one day someone will find it and read *A Christmas Carol* because of what you wrote!

• Story-before-the-Story

Marley must have liked his old partner. How did those two meet? Why did they become partners? What kind of business, exactly, did they have? What caused Marley's death? Write your own story—*Before A Christmas Carol*. See if you can create another character with a distinctive name.

• Into the Future

This report predicts what might happen if *A Christmas Carol* were to continue. It may take the form of a story in narrative or dramatic form or a visual display.

• A Letter to the Author

In this report you can write a letter to Charles Dickens. Tell him what you liked about *A Christmas Carol* and ask him any questions you may have about the writing of the book. You might want to give him some suggestions for a sequel! After your teacher has read it and you have made your writing the best it can be, read it to the class.

• Guess Who or What!

This report takes the form of several games of "Twenty Questions." The reporter gives a series of clues about a character from the story in a vague-to-precise, general-to-specific order. After all clues have been given, the identity of the mystery character must be deduced. After the character has been guessed, the same reporter presents another "Twenty Questions" about an event in the story.

• A Character Comes to Life

Suppose one of the characters in *A Christmas Carol* came to life and walked into your home or classroom. This report gives a view of what this character sees, hears, and feels as he or she experiences the modern world in which you live.

• Sales Talk

This report serves as an advertisement to "sell" *A Christmas Carol* to one or more specific groups. You decide on the group to target and the sales pitch you will use. Include some kind of graphics or visual aid in your presentation.

• Coming Attraction!

You have been chosen to design the promotional poster for *A Christmas Carol*, the movie. Include the title and author of the book, a listing of the main characters and the contemporary actors who will play them, a drawing of a scene from the book, and a paragraph synopsis of the story.

• Literary Interview

This report is done in pairs. One student will pretend to be a character in the story, steeped completely in the persona of his or her character. The other student will play the role of a television or radio interviewer, trying to provide the audience with insights into the character's personality and life. It is the responsibility of the partners to create meaningful questions and appropriate responses.

Research Ideas

Describe three things in *A Christmas Carol* that you want to learn more about.

_____

_____

_____

As you read *A Christmas Carol,* you encountered an earlier time, geographical location, social conditions, patterns of speech, and even a writing style that may seem unfamiliar to you. Understanding these things will help increase your appreciation of the book, Dickens' craft as a writer, and his concern for social problems.

Work in groups or on your own to research one or more of the areas you named above or the areas named below. Share your findings with the rest of the class in a project or report.

The London of 1800 to 1870

- Horse transport
- Heating
- Ladies' dress styles
- Childhood education
- Poverty
- Police protection
- Surgery
- Childhood diseases
- Pollution (air and water)
- London map
- Poorhouses
- Popular games
- Popular songs & music
- Well known actors & performers
- Common sayings, expressions, figures of speech

- Public and private lighting
- Gentlemen's dress styles
- Factory work
- Childhood work
- Crime
- Medicine
- Drug abuse
- Overcrowded housing
- Foods/diet/nutrition
- English writers and books
- Debtor's prison
- Popular dances
- Popular plays
- Popular holidays (other than Christmas)

From Humbug to Merry Christmas

Illustrate Scrooge's change from "Humbug" to "Merry Christmas." Scrooge, as all people do, showed his emotions on his face. Retell the story by drawing Scrooge's expression during each part of the story in the boxes below. Include an adjective to describe the expression.

(**Note to the teacher:** This activity could be completed as a review for the cause and effect test or as an alternate test.)

Let's Go Wassailing

In the 1800's people went wassailing. The practice of wassailing resembled our Christmas caroling. During the holiday season, groups of people carrying mugs of wassail walked through the town, singing traditional carols such as this one.

Here We Come A-Caroling
The Wassail Song (Traditional)

Here we come a-car-ol-ing a-mong the leaves so green;

Here we come a-wan-d'ring so fair — to be seen.

Chorus

Love and joy come to you, And to you glad Christ-mas

too, And God bless you and send ___ you a Hap — py New

Year, And God send you a Hap-py New ___ Year.

Wassail is a hot spicy cider that people used to toast one another's health. (Word history: The Anglo-Saxon words "Wae's hael" mean Be thou hail.) In Stave Three, Fred toasts his Uncle Scrooge with a mulled wine. ("Mull" means to warm and flavor with spices.)

To hold a Wassail Party, all you will need is a bowl of wassail (hot spiced cider) and Christmas carols. Students may toast one another with mugs of wassail and then carol through the school.

Mulled Apple Cider, Warm and Spicy

To make 32 (½ cup) servings:

1. Combine 1 gallon (4L) apple cider, 40 whole cloves, 1 tablespoon (15 mL) whole allspice, 2 - 5 cinnamon sticks, and ⅔ to 1 cup (236 mL) sugar.

   * Add cinnamon sticks and sugar to taste.

2. Bring mixture to a boil.

3. Cover and allow to simmer for 20 minutes.

4. Remove spices and pour into a punch bowl.

5. Garnish with whole oranges studded with cloves.

Novel Trivia Challenge

Materials: 2 or more teams, depending on class size. Trivia questions and answers based on the novel.

Preparation:

1. Form teams.

2. Working with partners on their teams, students write questions about the novel for the other teams to answer. The questions and answers should be literal or factual in nature, so any disputed answer may be checked in the text. Speculation or opinion questions do not work well in this game.

Directions:

1. The teacher acts as the game monitor and asks the questions to each team. The teacher also decides if the answer is correct and complete. If the question is answered correctly, the team is awarded one point. If a team cannot answer the question, the team that wrote the question is awarded one point. Questions may be answered in two ways: (1) each individual team member is given a turn to answer, or (2) the team works together to discuss the answer before it is given.

2. Play continues until all questions have been answered.

3. The members of the winning team are awarded certificates.

_____

was a member of the winning team

in the

𝔄 𝔊𝔥𝔯𝔦𝔰𝔱𝔪𝔞𝔰 𝔊𝔞𝔯𝔬𝔩

Trivia Challenge

Month _____ Day _____ Year _____

Congratulations on a job well-done and a novel well-read!

Judge _____

Cause and Effect

A Christmas Carol contains a series of events that cause the main character, Ebenezer Scrooge, to change.

Directions:

Complete the cause and effect chart below. Your list should be specific. Think through the events and characters Scrooge meets in the story. Note the event and explain its effect on Scrooge, or note the effect and explain the event that caused it. (Example: At the beginning of the story Scrooge is visited by his nephew, Fred. Fred wishes Scrooge a "Merry Christmas," and Scrooge becomes angry and explains how Christmas is a "Humbug." The causal event is the nephew's visit. The effect on Scrooge is anger and resentment toward his nephew and the Christmas season.)

Causes (story events) / Effects (changes in Scrooge, how Scrooge reacts)

Cause	*Effect*
1. Fred wishes Scrooge "Merry Christmas" and invites him to dinner.	*1. Scrooge becomes angry and replies, "Humbug!"*
2. Gentlemen come collecting for the poor.	2. _____
3. Bob Cratchit asks for Christmas day off.	3. _____
4. Scrooge sees himself as a child.	4. _____
5. Scrooge sees Belle's family life on Christmas.	5. _____
6. _____	6. Scrooge regrets his reaction to Bob Cratchit's request for Christmas off.
7. _____	7. Scrooge is saddened about his rejection of Fred.
8. _____	8. Scrooge feels sorry for Tiny Tim.
9. _____	9. Scrooge fears for his future.
10. _____	10. Scrooge raises Bob's salary and promises to help his family.

Response

Explain the meaning of these quotations from *A Christmas Carol*.

Stave One: Marley's Ghost

1. *'I wear the chain I forged in life,' replied the Ghost. 'I made it link by link, and yard by yard; I girded it on of my own free will, and of my own free will I wore it.'*

2. *'We choose this time because it is a time, of all others, when Want is keenly felt, and Abundance rejoices. What shall I put you down for?'*

Stave Two: The First of the Three Spirits

3. *'The school is not quite deserted,' said the Ghost. 'A solitary child, neglected by his friends, is left there still.' Scrooge said he knew it, and he sobbed.*

4. *'Yo ho, my boys, no more work tonight...Christmas Eve, Dick. Christmas, Ebenezer! Let's have the shutters up,' cried old Fezziwig, with a sharp clap of his hands, ' before a man can say Jack Robinson.'*

Stave Three: The Second of the Three Spirits

5. *'I am sorry for him; I couldn't be angry with him if I tried. Who suffers by his ill whims? Himself always. Here, he takes it into his head to dislike us, and he won't come and dine with us. What's the consequence?'*

6. *'I see a vacant seat...in the poor chimney corner, and a crutch without an owner carefully preserved. If these shadows remain unaltered by the Future, the child will die.'*

7. *Knocking down the fire irons, tumbling over the chairs, bumping up against the piano, smothering himself among the curtains, wherever she went, there went he! He always knew where the plump sister was.*

Stave Four: The Last of the Spirits

8. *'It's likely to be a very cheap funeral,' said the same speaker, ' for upon my life, I don't know of anybody to go to it. Suppose we make up a party and volunteer?'*

9. *'Spirit,' he cried, tight clutching at its robe, 'hear me! I am not the man I was. I will not be the man I must have been but for this intercourse. Why show me this if I am past all hope?'*

Stave Five: The End of It

10. *...and to Tiny Tim, who did not die, he was a second father. Some people laughed to see the alteration in him, but he let them laugh, and little heeded them, for he was wise enough to know that nothing ever happened on this globe for good, at which some people did not have their fill of laughter.*

Conversations

In size-appropriate groups write and perform the conversations that might have occurred in one of the following situations. If you wish, you may use your own conversation idea for the characters from *A Christmas Carol.*

- Marley and Scrooge as young men greedily plan to become rich as partners in business. *(2 persons)*

- Before they split up, Belle and Scrooge argue over whether to help a poor relative or invest their savings in gold. *(2 persons)*

- Fred and Bob Cratchit compare what they know about Scrooge, relating specific things the old skinflint has done over the years. *(2 persons)*

- After he is grown, Tiny Tim tells his own son a story about the boy's grandfather, Bob Cratchit. *(2 persons)*

- Mrs. Cratchit meets Scrooge on the street (before he changes) and lets him know just exactly what she thinks of him. He becomes very upset. *(2 persons)*

- Interviewing for a job with old Fezziwig, Bob Cratchit must explain that he wants to quit working for Scrooge and why. He does not know that Scrooge once worked for Fezziwig. *(2 persons)*

- Bob Cratchit tells a skeptical Mrs. Cratchit that Scrooge has offered to pay for special medical care for Tiny Tim. Mrs. Cratchit thinks there must be something wrong with the offer and argues with Bob. Peter and Martha join in the discussion. *(4 persons)*

- Tiny Tim explains to his own son how he knows that people can change and become better than they were. The boy's Aunt Belinda supports her brother's story. *(3 persons)*

- Marley talks with Cratchit, explaining what has happened to him—his death, the reason for his chains, etc. *(2 persons)*

- Scrooge recognizes Fezziwig (now much older) on the street and stops him to explain how much he now appreciates his old boss and why. *(2 persons)*

- Marley and the three Spirits meet after Christmas and discuss who they think was most successful in changing Scrooge. *(4 persons)*

- Fred, Tiny Tim, and Old Fezziwig discuss what they think is most important for a successful party. Remember what each seemed to enjoy the most. *(3 persons)*

- Mrs. Cratchit, Belle, and Fred's wife discuss how a husband's work conditions can affect their life at home. *(3 persons)*

- After the party at Fred's house, Fred, his wife, and her "plump sister" talk about Topper. Fred teases the sister a bit, but his wife thinks Topper would be a good match for her sister. *(3 persons)*

Bibliography of Related Reading

Cooper, Steve. *"A Dickens of a Christmas."* (Country Home, Vol. 11, pp. 82-86. Dec., 1989)
Curry, Jane L. *What the Dickens!* (Macmillan, 1991)
The Encyclopedia Americana, International Edition. (Grolier, Inc. Vol. 9, pp. 75-79, 1991)
Great Works of the English Language. (Marshall Cavendish Corporation, pp. 6-17, 1989)
The New Encyclopedia Britannica. (Encyclopedia Britannica, Inc., Vol. 17, pp. 267-273, 1985)
The Oxford Companion to English Literature. (Oxford University Press, pp. 272-273, 1985)
Stanley, Diane and Vennema, Peter. *Charles Dickens: The Man Who Had Great Expectations.* (Morrow Junior Books, 1993)

Other Books by Charles Dickens

David Copperfield. (Penguin, 1966)
Great Expectations. (Bantam, 1985)
Oliver Twist. (NAL, 1961)
Tale of Two Cities. (Dodd, 1985)

Other Stories about Christmas

Barth, Edna, ed. *A Christmas Feast: Poems, Sayings, Greetings, and Wishes.* (Clarion, 1979)
Batchelor, Mary. *Our Family Christmas Book.* (Abingdon, 1984)
Herda, D.J. *Christmas.* (Watts, 1983)
Livingston, Myra Cohn, ed. *Poems of Christmas.* (Macmillan, 1980)

Other Stories about Victorian England

Aiken, Joan. *Midnight Is a Place.* (Viking, 1974)
Garfield, Leon. *The December Rose.* (Viking, 1987)
Garfield, Leon. *The Empty Sleeve.* (Doubleday, 1988)
Garfield, Leon. *Footsteps.* (Delacorte, 1980)
Green, Roger J. *The Throttlepenny Murder.* (Oxford Press, 1989)
Newman, Robert. *The Case of the Murdered Players.* (Macmillan, 1985)
Newman, Robert. *The Case of the Watching Boy.* (Macmillan, 1987)
Sewall, Anna. *Black Beauty.* (Airmont, 1974)

Related Videos

A Christmas Carol. There are several versions of this title available, including the following:
  A Christmas Carol. MGM/UA, 1938
  A Christmas Carol. United Entertainment, Inc., 1951
  A Christmas Carol. Rhino Home Video, 1969 (animated)
  A Christmas Carol. American School Pub., 1982
  A Christmas Carol. Childrens Video Library, 1983 (animated)

Scrooge. The following versions of this title are available:
  Scrooge. Video Yesteryear, 1935
  Scrooge. Video Communications, Inc., 1951
  Scrooge. Fox Video, 1970 (musical)

An American Christmas Carol. Vestron Video, 1979
Mr. McGoo's Christmas Carol. Paramount Home Video, 1964
Mickey's Christmas Carol. Walt Disney Home Video, 1983

Answer Key

Page 10, Part One

1. Accept appropriate responses.
2. Scrooge works in a counting-house, candles are used to light windows, burned coal for heat, office is referred to as the "tank," Parliament, debtor's prison, workhouses, poulterers, etc.
3. Other characters: Fred—Scrooge's nephew; Bob Cratchit—Scrooge's employee; men collecting for the poor—businessmen in town; Marley—Scrooge's deceased partner.
4. Rooms, furnishings, clothes, actions were bare and frugal.
5. Accept appropriate responses.
6. Accept appropriate responses.

Page 10, Part Two

1. Marley is Scrooge's deceased friend. Marley was Scrooge's business partner.
2. Marley's purpose is to warn Scrooge of his fate if he does not change his ways and of the coming of the Spirits.
3. Both are businessmen, greedy, only friends each other had, wealthy, neither celebrated Christmas.
4. Marley and Scrooge are different: Marley knows the value in helping others, Scrooge sees no reason to help others, Marley is dead.
5. Moaning, clanking chains, ringing bells, door knocker, flames in fireplace leap up.

Page 12, Part One

1. Stingy, greedy, tight-fisted: refuses to donate to the poor, does not pay his employees well; does not celebrate Christmas; unfriendly: refuses to visit his nephew; good businessman: owns a business; lonely: has no friends or companions; cold hearted: throws a ruler at the Christmas caroler.
2. Accumulation of wealth.
3. Accept appropriate responses.
4. Accept appropriate responses.

Page 12, Part Two

1. Purpose of the ringing bell is to get Scrooge's attention.
2. Marley visits Scrooge to warn Scrooge about his fate. Marley is a true friend to Scrooge.
3. The chain represents the mean things he did in his life. A chain is formed by ignoring the needs of others.
4. Scrooge is frightened by the chain and the vision of the moaning ghosts.
5. As a ghost, Marley must wander the earth witnessing the unhappiness of others. He tries to advise the person, but he is unable to make any difference.
6. Scrooge learns that what people do in their life affects their fate after they die.

Page 15

1. Spirit one resembles a small child but with white hair, white tunic, holding green holly, tunic trimmed in flowers, bright light streaming from his head.
2. He regrets not giving something to the small boy who sang for him earlier in the day.
3. The Spirit says that she married, died, and left a child—Scrooge's nephew.
4. Scrooge defends his old boss: "The happiness he gives is quite as great as if it cost a fortune." He regrets his treatment of his clerk, Cratchit.
5. Scrooge witnesses loving children, laughter, noise, happiness, as Belle's husband returns with gifts and toys for all.

Page 18

1. The light represents the light of the holiday season.
2. The light would be hidden by unkind acts—wars, crime, cruelty, mean words, and teasing.
3. The Spirit came to save Scrooge and improve his life. Initially, Scrooge does not like the Spirit and does not want to go with it.
4. The schoolboy Scrooge is sensitive and timid; apprentice Scrooge is friendly and fun loving; The adult Scrooge is greedy and eager to gain wealth.

Answer Key (cont.)

5. Scrooge decided poverty was a terrible condition and begins to work very hard to gain wealth.

6. As a young boy Scrooge was left alone at boarding school during Christmas, and later in his life his girlfriend leaves him.

Page 21

1. A jolly giant with brown hair, great torch, deep green robe lined with white fur, bare feet, holly wreath on head, icicles, sparkling eyes, antique scabbard without a sword.

2. The Ghost has white hair at the end.

3. The Cratchit home was poor, with children Peter, Martha, a small boy and girl, Tiny Tim with his crutch. The dinner was goose with potatoes, plum pudding, gravy.

4. The party had laughter, harp music, games of Blind Man's Buff, Yes & No, and How, When, and Where.

5. Cratchit & Fred act kindly, offering toasts in the spirit of Christmas. The families are not at all so kind but are finally accepting for the sake of Christmas.

Page 23

1. He does not celebrate Christmas.

2. The Spirit takes Scrooge to Cratchit's house, his nephew's house, and throughout the town and countryside.

3. He does not celebrate Christmas.

4. Mrs. Cratchit is angry because she knows how hard her husband works and he is not compensated for his hard work. She sees all the things her family cannot have, and she knows Scrooge is rich and greedy.

5. Scrooge enjoys playing the party games and asks the Spirit if they can stay longer.

6. The Spirit is aging because Christmas Present is coming to an end.

Page 24

1. And so as Tiny Tim observed, God bless us every one.

2. –••• •– ••••/••• •– •• –••/••• –•– •–• ––– ––– ––• •/

   •••• ••– –– –••• ••– ––•/

3. (a) Spirit One (b) Scrooge (c) Scrooge

Page 26

1. Spirit One reminds him of his past and how he enjoyed people and had fun. Spirit Two teaches him what he is missing by rejecting people and living alone. Spirit Three teaches Scrooge that his death will not be treated with kindness, and no one will remember him.

2. To show how a person changes throughout his life.

3. Spirit Three was the most frightening because Scrooge had no idea how awful his future would be.

4. Accept appropriate responses.

5. Accept appropriate responses.

Page 28

1. Scrooge means he has changed because the Spirits have shown him the man he was and what he is missing in his life.

2. The final experience teaches Scrooge his vision of himself is different from the view others have of him.

3. He sees how his business practices left him without friends or human kindness at his death. He was not recognized for anything good by his peers.

4. Accept appropriate responses.

5. The Spirits have shown Scrooge that honoring Christmas means helping people in need. He vows to change his greedy attitude to a generous attitude.

6. Accept appropriate responses.

Page 31

1. Scrooge is described as laughing, saying a kind word to everyone, dancing around, buying a turkey for the Cratchits, giving money to the poor, visiting his nephew, etc.

2. The weather is clear and bright, not foggy and cloudy.

3. The Spirits were successful because they reminded Scrooge of his past and showed him a future he never considered.

Answer Key *(cont.)*

4. Scrooge is sincere because he gives to the poor, visits his nephew, and promises to help Bob Cratchit.

5. Accept appropriate responses.

6. Accept appropriate responses.

Page 33

1. Spirit One reminds him of his past and how he enjoyed people and had fun. Spirit Two teaches him what he is missing by rejecting people and living alone. Spirit Three teaches Scrooge that his death will not be treated with kindness, and no one will remember him.

2. Scrooge is anxious to begin changing his life. He could not make decisions or choices during the Spirits' visitations.

3. He displays emotions (joy and sadness); he dances; he speaks kindly to others; he generously gives to others.

4. Scrooge has new feelings for the door knocker because that is how Marley first appeared to Scrooge and started his adventure with the Spirits.

5. Blithe means joyous. Synonyms are wonderful, happy, excellent, exuberant, etc.

6. Accept appropriate responses.

7. Fred has grown up with his Uncle Scrooge and may remember how his uncle acted when Scrooge was younger. Bob only knows Scrooge as his boss, and Scrooge's new behavior is inconsistent with the boss he remembers.

Page 39

Accept appropriate responses. Examples:

Part One: Adjectives: angry, mad, bothered. Causes: nephew, gentlemen, Cratchit.

Part Two: Adjectives: shocked, afraid, surprised. Causes: door knocker, ringing bell, Marley, the chains.

Part Three: Adjectives: sorrowful, guilty, self-pitying. Causes: boarding school, Fezziwig's warehouse, girlfriend.

Part Four: Adjectives: sad, happy at the party, concerned for the Cratchits. Causes: learning about Tiny Tim's illness, nephew's party, seeing

others celebrating Christmas.

Part Five: Adjectives: miserable, self pitying, fearful. Causes: he sees his death and realizes no one will miss him.

Part Six: Adjectives: happy, excited, silly. Causes: the visitation and the lessons of the Spirits.

Page 42

Accept appropriate responses. Examples:

1. Cause: Fred's visit and invitation to Christmas dinner, Effect: anger and resentment toward his nephew and Christmas

2. Effect: anger—shows he is not responsible for others.

3. Effect: feels Bob's request is unreasonable and paying him for vacation is unfair.

4. Effect: regrets not being kind to the boy who stopped to sing him a carol.

5. Effect: regrets deeply the loss of his girlfriend, lost because of his greed.

6. Cause: Scrooge has seen how generous and outgoing Fezziwig was to his employees.

7. Cause: Scrooge has seen how Fred really does like him and wants nothing in return.

8. Cause: Scrooge sees the simple joys of the poor Cratchit family and how much they love the crippled boy.

9. Cause: Spirit Three has shown him the grim aftermath of his own death.

10. Cause: He has awakened a new man, reformed and sympathetic to others.

Page 43

Accept appropriate responses.

Page 44

Accept appropriate responses.